12 Simple Truths for Living and Loving Yourself

A Journey of Self-Reflection and Self-Discovery for Women and Girls

By: Lisa Lynch, M.Ed., Ed.S.

12 Simple Truths for Living and Loving Yourself

A Journey of Self-Reflection and Self-Discovery for Women and Girls

12 Simple Truths for Living and Loving Yourself

Copyright © 2021 Lisa Lynch

ALL RIGHTS RESERVED. This book contains material protected under International and Federal Copyright Laws and Treaties. Any unauthorized reprint or use of this material is prohibited. No part of this book may be reproduced or transmitted in any form or by any means, electronic or mechanical, including photocopying, recording, or by any information storage and retrieval system without express written permission from the author/publisher.

Unless otherwise noted all Scripture quotations are taken from the New International Version of the Bible. All rights reserved.

Scripture taken from the New International Version®.

Copyright © 1978 by Biblica. Used by permission. All rights reserved.

Book Cover Design: Jada A. Lynch

Printed by: Prize Publishing House, LLC in the United States of America.

First printing edition 2021.

Prize Publishing House

P.O. Box 9856, Chesapeake, VA 23321

www.PrizePublishingHouse.com

ISBN (Paperback): 978-1-7371829-4-8

ISBN (E-Book): 978-1-7371829-1-7

12 Simple Truths for Living and Loving Yourself

Table of Contents

Endorsements..iii

Dedication iv

Foreword v

Focus on Your Faith 6

Don't Underestimate Your Strength........................... 15

Be Your Own Champion...23

Teach People How to Treat You 31

Discover Your Purpose and Passion...........................39

Choose Your Inner Circle of Friends Wisely 48

Empower Other Women and Girls.............................56

Know Your Worth..65

Practice Self-Discipline...73

Speak Your Truth 82

Seek Peace and Justice for All 89

Be the Best Version of Yourself 98

Endorsements

This amazing journal of self-reflection and self-discovery is full of God's empowering promises that will thrust women and girls into becoming just who God created them to be. Every truth Lisa has penned in this journal is to help us LIVE...LOVE...and LEARN more about ourselves, each other, and life. It's a must-read for every woman and girl or mother and daughter who seeks being authentic in their relationship with God and each other. When you read it, her passion for us as women and girls to become who God called us to be leaps from the pages and transfers into our spirits. It's obvious she has lived through self-reflection and self-discovery.

Dr. Angela L. Corprew-Boyd, National Preacher, Teacher, Author & Leadership Consultant Women Empowered, Inc.

The Book 12 Simple Truths for Living and Loving Yourself is an empowering and insightful workbook for women of all ages who care deeply about their faith, future, and fulfillment in life.

Robin Turner, Author of They Dream in Darkness

Dedication

This book is dedicated to my precious mother, Catherine, my daughters, Taylor, Jada, and Mya, my mother-figures, aunties, cousins, sister-friends, nieces, and great-nieces, and the memories of my grandmothers, Dora and Millicent. These women and girls, along with the living spirits of my ancestors, mean *everything* to me. Their collective embodiment of strength, faith, beauty, intelligence, resilience, creativity, devotion, and tenacity through the countless ups, downs, twists and turns of life inspires me to live my life grounded by my faith in God with purpose, poise, dignity, and confidence.

Foreword

Dear Reader,

This book is a work of love that was birthed through reflecting on my own life and 25 years of experience as an educator. As I considered the next generation, I began to ponder what younger women might need to successfully navigate through life and how lessons from my journey could serve them. My responsibility as an elder – especially as the mother of three incredible daughters and an aunt and great-aunt to precious nieces – is to set an example for living a fulfilling life grounded in faith and self-love. It is my desire to inspire women and girls like you to live purposefully in alignment with God's plan while unapologetically embracing your beauty, power, and brilliance. It's all about living, loving, growing, and glowing so that our lights can shine for others to see our good deeds and glorify the Father in heaven.

This book takes the form of a guided journal. It is designed to encourage self-love, self-reflection, and self-discovery through the 12 simple, but universal truths and help you chronicle the journey.

Lisa Lynch

12 Simple Truths for Living and Loving Yourself

01

Focus on Your Faith

"...so that your faith might not rest on human wisdom, but on God's power."

1 Corinthians 2:5 (NIV)

Live. Love. Grow. Glow.

The values and standards that we hold in our hearts and minds to guide our lives should reflect our belief in the only unchanging, ever-present, all-powerful God. He has graciously outlined fundamental principles for us in His instruction manual for life, the Bible. As human beings, we are imperfect, yet we often look to one another to get our needs met. The truth is that every person is flawed and in search of answers, direction, healing, happiness, and peace. God, on the other hand, is perfect, all-knowing, and the source of comfort and peace. We have to start with God and then look to those who are wiser than ourselves. We must learn to trust God more than people and develop a level of faith that can sustain us through the ups and downs and twists and turns of life. If we are to fulfill our true purpose and live a life that is pleasing to our Heavenly Father and grounded in faith, diligent study of God's word is essential. We have to find out what God says and wants for His children and let the Word take root in our hearts and minds.

As I look back on my life, I am so thankful for the lessons I learned as a child in Sunday School and church, although in my early years I was much more interested in the social aspect rather than biblical teachings. We were taught the Golden Rule, to be salt and light, and to keep God first in our lives. Our teachers told us God loves us and would always be with us. They taught us that God would forgive our sins if we accepted His gift of salvation through His son, Jesus Christ. We sang songs about the solid rock, blessed assurance, and letting our little lights shine. What I did not know in those early years was just how much I would come to rely on those teachings for direction and survival. I thank God today that those seeds of faith in a present and loving God were planted in my mind, body, and soul so early in my life. The lessons I learned provided the foundation I needed to discern right from wrong and understand my purpose and place in the world. Those teachings helped me navigate relationships, dodge the pitfalls of my teen and young adult years, and seek forgiveness when I failed at each. I am a long way from being that little girl, or young adult for that matter, but those songs, sermons, and Sunday School lessons remain central to my existence.

As an adult, I have been pushed to my limit more times than I can count. The blessing in all of it was that every challenge I faced nudged me closer to God and increased my faith. I find strength in knowing that the Creator cares about what I care about. He knows me and loves me still. God truly is the Solid Rock, and as I reflect on my journey and the relationship I have developed with my Lord and Savior I see His unseen hand in every experience. While I am grateful for my many blessings and the grace and mercy God has shown me time and time again, my faith continues to grow most when I go to God in prayer and trust Him with my pain, fears, and concerns. In doing so, I get to witness how He works things out for my good, even when I am not able to see how my tests could ever become my testimony. I can always find peace and the answers I need to continue my journey when I rely on God. I wish every woman and girl had those seeds of faith planted early in their lives, but that is not the reality for everyone. The great thing about God is that as long as there is breath in our bodies, there is hope. Every day that we wake up on this side of eternity is an opportunity to grow closer to the Lord and plant seeds of love and faith into others to inspire them to do the same.

We each have our own set of experiences and lessons to learn during our short time here on Earth. Though my journey looks and feels different from yours, our journeys come together through our connection as children of God. It is not by coincidence that you are reading this book. Like everything else in our lives, this too was divinely orchestrated with the greater purpose of drawing God's children closer together and increasing our faith and reliance on Him.

01 – Focus on Your Faith

Journal Prompt #1: *Describe your relationship with God and how you demonstrate faith in Him. Set a goal that you would like to achieve with God in one month.*

Date: _____

01 – Focus on Your Faith

Journal Prompt #2: *What does it mean to trust God completely? In what areas of life do you need to trust Him more?*

Date: _____

01 – Focus on Your Faith

Journal Prompt #3: *Assess the areas where you have planted seeds of love and hope. Have you seen any life spring forth yet? If not, where is God asking you to plant?*

Date: _____

01 – Focus on Your Faith

One Month Check-In

Self-reflection and self-discovery are ongoing processes. Use the space below to add a one-month update on your journey.

Date: _____

_____
_____
_____
_____
_____
_____
_____
_____
_____
_____
_____
_____
_____
_____
_____
_____

12 Simple Truths for Living and Loving Yourself

02

Don't Underestimate Your Strength

"I can do all this through Him who gives me strength."

Philippians 4:13 (NIV)

Live. Love. Grow. Glow.

Have you ever found yourself in a situation where you just dreaded having to see someone you preferred to avoid, go somewhere you did not want to go or deal with a situation you did not want to face? You likely felt uncomfortable, afraid, unprepared, or inadequate. My guess is that you could not avoid the person or situation and eventually had to deal with it despite your reservations. I have found that it is often in these uncomfortable places of internal conflict where we find out how strong and capable we really are. The truth is, those experiences are pruning, pressing, and stretching us. This process does not occur to make our lives miserable; it happens so that we can learn to trust God more and become the children He intended us to be. Life is splattered with obstacles and situations that will test us and our faith. We need to expect to encounter these opportunities for personal growth that will ultimately equip us with the knowledge, tools, and skills we need for the next stages of our journey. We are more prepared than we realize for every season of our lives, so we should not underestimate our strength.

Let's be honest, life can be hard and scary sometimes, but we are more prepared and much stronger than we give ourselves credit for. Sometimes our challenges and the burdens we carry get so heavy they can bring even the strongest, most courageous person to their knees in surrender. The loss of a loved one, abuse, homelessness, racism, illness, neglect, addiction, unemployment or underemployment, and countless other tragedies can happen at any time. No one is immune from hard times. When our journeys get to be too overwhelming, leaving us feeling lost, empty, and without hope, strength often comes from the support of loved ones and individuals who have our best interest at heart (such as a pastor or professional counselor). A person whose spirit is broken cannot be her own source of strength and healing. We all need help sometimes, which does not indicate that we are weaker or less capable than anyone else. It just means that our journeys, needs, and pathways are different. In good times and in bad times, we must lean into our faith, trust God, grant ourselves grace, and accept our humanity. God knows what we need and just how much we can handle. He is waiting for us to call to Him and ask for the help, peace, and power we need for the journey that only God can provide.

Excellence and power are in our DNA. The blood that runs through our veins is the same blood that flowed through the veins of our ancestors, who were powerful and remarkably gifted kings, queens, warriors, educators, architects, artisans, scientists, and mathematicians. We are descendants of beautiful people who were driven by an unconquerable spirit and will, and the kind of faith that compelled Harriet Tubman to serve as conductor for the Underground Railroad. We are capable of achieving the goals we set for ourselves if we do the hard work and make the necessary sacrifices. We must dream big dreams and follow God's plan for our lives. Nothing can stop a made-up mind. Consider the story of Sojourner Truth, the daughter of slaves and a slave herself who, propelled by her faith, became a preacher, abolitionist, and women's rights activist during a time in history when this was unheard of and extremely dangerous. What we do should not be motivated by our own will, nor should it be only for ourselves. We must commit our plans to the Lord and acknowledge God as the source of our strength.

02 – Don't Underestimate Your Strength

Journal Prompt #1: *Reflect on some of your most difficult life experiences and how you overcame them. Set a goal for overcoming a current challenge that you would like to achieve in one month.*

Date: _____

_____
_____
_____
_____
_____
_____
_____
_____
_____
_____
_____
_____
_____
_____
_____
_____

02 – Don't Underestimate Your Strength

Journal Prompt #2: *Describe a few times when you felt fearful or believed you were not strong enough to do something, yet you persevered despite those feelings and were surprised by your own strength.*

Date: _____

02 – Don't Underestimate Your Strength

Journal Prompt #3: *Who is your hero? What underlying qualities does that person possess that resonate with you, and how can you further develop those qualities in your own life?*

Date: _____

02 – Don't Underestimate Your Strength

One Month Check-In

Self-reflection and self-discovery are ongoing processes. Use the space below to add a one-month update on your journey.

Date: _____

_____
_____
_____
_____
_____
_____
_____
_____
_____
_____
_____
_____
_____
_____
_____
_____

12 Simple Truths for Living and Loving Yourself

03

Be Your Own Champion

"Have I not commanded you? Be strong and courageous. Do not be afraid; do not be discouraged, for the Lord your God will be with you wherever you go."

Joshua 1:9 (NIV)

Live. Love. Grow. Glow.

When we think of the word champion, certain images seem to immediately come to mind of athletes celebrating a home run, slam dunk, Super Bowl win, or victory in the World Cup. We must expand the definition of what a champion is and learn to be our own champions. Far too often we look to others as idols or icons and downplay our own efforts, contributions, and achievements. Of course, it would be great if we could swing a racket like Serena, belt out songs and woo crowds like Beyonce', rip the fashion runway like Rihanna, or flow like the National Youth Poet Laureate, Amanda Gorman, but these are their stories and not ours. When we become our own champions, we learn to encourage ourselves with a little pep-talk, celebration, or pat on the back. Once we understand that we simply have to do our best in the space we are in until we can do better, we will begin to see ourselves as worthy players in the proverbial game.

It begins with routinely setting short and long-term goals and adjusting and pivoting in another direction if life requires us to do so. We have to learn to be our own sunshine on some of those dark days and recognize that mistakes and missteps are inevitable parts of our growth process. Life is unpredictable, and things are happening that are beyond our control all the time. Champions keep fighting when times get hard. They work diligently to perfect their craft and do the best they possibly can in any given set of circumstances. They understand their purpose and cause even others around them to rise to every occasion. Every challenge we encounter along our journey through life is an opportunity to lean more on our faith, to overcome the obstacles before us and demonstrate perseverance and endurance. All of these traits are further developed as we work through the power of God within us.

We must learn to celebrate our baby steps and the great and small achievements we make as we move through the stages of life. As we keep living, learning, and moving forward toward the end goal, we will continue to grow personally and professionally and inspire ourselves and others in the process. Yes, we are each champions in our own right, deserving of praise and adoration as we let our lights shine so that others will see God in us and glorify Him. Let's face it though, bad things can happen to good people just as good things can happen to good people. This is a reality of life that every one of us has to accept. Life is a journey, and we will be pushed beyond what we consider to be our limits, but much like a diamond, the pressure will eventually reveal our brilliance and the champion that lives within all of us. When facing tough times, we have three choices: give up, give in, or give it to God.

One of the greatest gifts I give myself is permission to be me. I have learned not to measure my progress and impact in the world against someone else's. My only competition stares back at me when I look in the mirror. I find that I am the best version of myself when I compare my yesterday or yesteryear self with who I am today. Spending time with family and friends who encourage and inspire me to be my best, praying, and practicing yoga help me to press the pause button, tune out the world, settle my thoughts, and tune into the Holy Spirit. This quiet time enables me to recenter, revisit my goals and divine purpose, and remember the God I serve.

03 – Be Your Own Champion

Journal Prompt #1: *What caught your attention in this chapter? Set a goal that you would like to achieve in one month as you become your own champion.*

Date: _____

_____
_____
_____
_____
_____
_____
_____
_____
_____
_____
_____
_____
_____
_____
_____
_____
_____
_____
_____

03 – Be Your Own Champion

Journal Prompt #2: *What advice would you give someone who does not see herself as a champion and is immobilized by fear, failure, rejection, or past hurts? How can you apply that advice to your life?*

Date: _____

_____
_____
_____
_____
_____
_____
_____
_____
_____
_____
_____
_____
_____
_____
_____
_____
_____
_____

03 – Be Your Own Champion

Journal Prompt #3: *Write positive affirmations to champion (encourage) yourself in this season.*

Date: _____

03 – Be Your Own Champion

One Month Check-In

Self-reflection and self-discovery are ongoing processes. Use the space below to add a one-month update on your journey.

Date: _____

12 Simple Truths for Living and Loving Yourself

04

Teach People How to Treat You

"I praise You because I am fearfully and wonderfully made; Your works are wonderful, I know that full well."

Psalm 139:14 (NIV)

Live. Love. Grow. Glow.

We are all children of the supreme God and Creator of all things. We must always be mindful of who and whose we are and to whom we will ultimately answer. We are unique, valued, and loved and should expect to be treated accordingly. God desires His children to be treated with dignity and respect and to treat others in the same manner. It is not God's will for dignity and respect to be portioned out according to our employer, social status, race, gender, age, or how much money we have in our bank accounts. God knows our worth because He made us in His own image and loves us unconditionally. We are all God's children, but we too must believe that our lives matter and have value and a divine purpose.

We have to learn to treat others as we wish to be treated and invite people into our lives who treat us as children of the King of Kings. We teach people how to treat us by the way we respond to their actions and by the manner in which we conduct ourselves. We must take inventory of our word choices and tone. Do we use offensive language or a hostile tone when we are speaking? Do we monitor our posture and the other ways we communicate nonverbally? Do we sit upright and stand straight or do we slump or slouch? Do we avoid eye contact or look people in the eye and nod to indicate that the message is being received? Do we refer to people by their names? Do we expect the same treatment? When we find ourselves being treated in a manner that does not demonstrate respect or honor towards us as children of God, we have to say or do something that leads to a common understanding of what is acceptable and what is not. We have to identify the issue with the individual or individuals and teach them what we prefer them to do or say in the future. When we accept abuse, neglect, and other forms of mistreatment, whether it is verbal or physical, we are teaching people that it is permissible to treat us that way.

Equally, when we establish and enforce boundaries, we are teaching people how to treat us. There are many reasons why we may find ourselves in unhealthy situations, but what is most important is that we use boundaries to limit exposure or remove ourselves from those harmful people and places. We must take some time to look around our village at those with whom we are in close community. We need to think about how they treat us and speak to us and ask ourselves if they truly honor and protect our dignity. Do they encourage us and value our lives and contributions? Our honest, thoughtful reflections may prompt us to have conversations with some individuals about changes that need to be made in order for us to remain in healthy relationship with one another.

It is not ideal, and conflict is never easy, but we may need to disinvite some people from being a regular part of our lives until they can learn how to treat us. We have the power to teach people how to treat us and should never forget that we are God's beloved children. He created us, and that alone makes us worthy of love, dignity, and proper treatment.

04 – Teach People How to Treat You

Journal Prompt #1: *When you look in the mirror at who God created, what do you see? Do you see someone who is lovable and worthy of respect? Set a goal around the theme of loving yourself that you would like to achieve in one month.*

Date: _____

04 – Teach People How to Treat You

Journal Prompt #2: *What does respect look and sound like for you? How can you be more intentional about demonstrating respect towards others as you wish to have it demonstrated towards you?*

Date: _____

04 – Teach People How to Treat You

Journal Prompt #3: *Are there any areas where you need to establish boundaries? What steps will you take to implement them?*

Date: _____

04 – Teach People How to Treat You

One Month Check-In

Self-reflection and self-discovery are ongoing processes. Use the space below to add a one-month update on your journey.

Date: _____

_____
_____
_____
_____
_____
_____
_____
_____
_____
_____
_____
_____
_____
_____
_____
_____
_____

12 Simple Truths for Living and Loving Yourself

12 Simple Truths for Living and Loving Yourself

05

Discover Your Purpose and Passion

"Each of you should use whatever gift you have received to serve others, as faithful stewards of God's grace in its various forms."

1 Peter 4:10 (NIV)

Live. Love. Grow. Glow.

We are all blessed by God with specific gifts and talents, and it is our responsibility while on Earth to discover and use those gifts and talents to be of service to others. As we do so, we bring glory to God and can inspire the people around us to accept God's gift of salvation through Jesus Christ. We are called to make a positive difference in the world, which is not only true for a select group, but for every one of us. We can all serve and contribute in some way, whether with time, money, ideas, encouragement, or prayers. The goal is to serve our families, communities, and the world in some positive way, small or large, direct or indirect. It will make an impact.

We are sometimes unsure of what our gifts and talents are or do not know where to begin, which often keeps us from doing anything. The answer is to start with the places and spaces we occupy each day. God has placed us in these places and spaces for a divine purpose. We must consider our work environment and co-workers. Who might be sad, hurt, confused, or lonely and just needs a little encouragement, acknowledgment, or support? Who in our church family is sick, bereaved, or struggling? Think about your immediate community. Who could use a kind word, a smile, encouragement, resources we can provide, or some of our undivided time and attention? Think about the other places you frequent, such as the grocery store, salon, and school. There are people in need all around us waiting for us to open our hearts and minds and use our gifts and talents to serve and supply their emotional, physical, and spiritual needs.

When I have an opportunity to speak with others about my work, I share with them that I consider being an educator my ministry. Educators are inherently in a position to impart wisdom and give hope, inspiration, encouragement, and guidance to children and adults every day. I have found that lending a smile, kind words, compassion, patience, persistence, resources, or support in decision making can shift a child or adult's thought patterns from despair to hope and their self-perception from limitations to endless potential. That shift has a ripple effect which eventually has a positive impact on peers, family members, and the global community.

Yes, the law requires separation of Church and State, but I find that when God's Spirit lives in us and our passions and purpose align with His will, others can feel a special kind of warmth and see that there is something different about us, even in the school setting. There is a glow that is undeniable and at times inexplicable. The Holy Spirit within us permeates everything around us and can be heard, seen, and felt in our words, our conduct, and our interactions. I consider it a blessing and God's work to be able to bring light and enlightenment to the lives of the children and adults I have had the honor of serving. We all must learn to take notice of the people we encounter, survey their needs, and see beyond their external persona. When we see needs or opportunities to serve and inspire others, we must take advantage of them. As we do so, we are using our gifts and talents in the way God intended for them to be used, to fuel our passions and purpose.

God called His followers to be salt and light on the Earth. He chose salt because it is a natural element that preserves and keeps things from going bad. Salt is a change agent that enhances the space it occupies. Through the Holy Spirit, we too can be influencers, change-makers, and enhancers. We must discover what brings us joy and peace and what we do best because that is where our passion can be found. Next, we have to determine how we can fulfill our purpose and make a positive impact in our frequented spaces. There is darkness, evil, and chaos all around us and the only way to rid spaces of darkness is by bringing in some light. We, the children of God, are the light the world needs right now. We must devote our lives to honoring God, using the gifts and talents with which we have been blessed to discover our purpose. For those of us who are still trying to figure out our purpose and determine what we are passionate about, take some time to quiet the mind and focus inward more often. That inner voice, the Spirit, typically tugs at us urging us to move towards someone or something. That is the place or space where we can start using our gifts and talents for God's glory.

We also need to consider the lessons in our stories that connect the journey behind us and before us. Our struggles and achievements are powerful and purposeful and can be used to help someone else if we are willing to share our experiences and the lessons we learned along the way. Other women and girls need to know how we got out of our dark places, persevered through hard times, and attained a level of success they aspire to achieve. We must learn to listen to what the Holy Spirit is saying to us about our purpose and passions.

05 – Discover Your Purpose and Passion

Journal Prompt #1: *What brings you happiness and makes you feel fulfilled? What are you good at and enjoy doing? How can you use your gifts, talents, and those things that bring you joy to aid and uplift others in your family and community? Set a goal that you would like to achieve in one month.*

Date: _____

05 – Discover Your Purpose and Passion

Journal Prompt #2: *What are the highlights of your story? How can you use your story to inspire others in everyday life?*

Date: _____

05 – Discover Your Purpose and Passion

Journal Prompt #3: *What are some practical ways that you can bring light to the dark places around you?*

Date: _____

05 – Discover Your Purpose and Passion

One Month Check-In

Self-reflection and self-discovery are ongoing processes. Use the space below to add a one-month update on your journey.

Date: _____

_____
_____
_____
_____
_____
_____
_____
_____
_____
_____
_____
_____
_____

12 Simple Truths for Living and Loving Yourself

06

Choose Your Inner Circle of Friends Wisely

"Perfume and incense bring joy to the heart, and the pleasantness of a friend springs from their heartfelt advice."

Proverbs 27:9 (NIV)

Live. Love. Grow. Glow.

Life is not meant to be lived in isolation from other people. A life free of isolation requires that we learn to balance being independent while acknowledging the importance of interdependency, or reliance on one another. A circle of friends who support, motivate, nurture, and challenge us to be our best is essential for personal growth and accountability. Those individuals we invite into our inner circles should help us smile brighter, laugh harder, and love ourselves more. After God, they should be the first people to whom we look to share our joys and pains. We feel safe opening up and having honest conversations with them. They have seen us at our best and worst and love us still. We can count on our inner circle of friends to provide a safe and soft place to fall and rest or give us that spark we need to keep living, learning, growing, and moving forward when we need it. We all need that special group of friends who complement us, are fun to be around and talk to, are available, and who demonstrate the character traits we value.

Some friends will enter and exit our lives rather quickly, while others enter and remain for the duration of our journey. It is often not due to a failure or something lacking on our part when friendships end or fizzle away. Each person we encounter on our journey has a purpose, to show us something, tell us something, or reveal something about ourselves. We have to live and learn the lessons they showed up to teach us, recognizing that God orchestrated our paths crossing.

Our closest circle of friends are the ones who will be with us for the long haul. They consistently demonstrate compassion and honesty without judgment, often aid us in the process of discovering God's will and purpose for our lives. Our inner circle of friends also serves as our own personal mirrors that reflect our present selves and the vision we have for our futures. From time to time, we need to take a closer look at our friends and take inventory so that we can be sure we are sharing joys, pains, fears, and aspirations with people who can be trusted to protect and guide us in the right direction. Our inner circle of friends reflects our values, beliefs, and goals.

In this crazy digital world, it is more important now than ever to be careful who we call a friend and allow in our inner circles. We must not confuse friends with our followers, fans, and associates. Sometimes we can get so focused on how many friends we have and how many people like us that we lose sight of why we have allowed people who may not have our best interests at heart to become closer to us than they probably should be. We must be certain of the intentions of those we call a friend and ensure that those individuals are worthy of our time, dedication, and friendship. True friends are present and reliable, loving us despite our flaws and enriching our lives. They are not solely focused on their own interests. Most importantly, they draw us closer to God and not further away from Him and His will for our lives, and we do the same for them. We must live in community with others, but we must also be particularly careful when choosing whom we allow in our inner circles because, "Bad company corrupts good character," according to 1 Corinthians 15:33.

06 – Choose Your Inner Circle of Friends Wisely

Journal Prompt #1: *Who is in your inner circle of friends and why? What values, beliefs, and goals do you have in common? Describe how your friends reflect who you are and aspire to be. Set a goal that you would like to achieve in one month.*

Date: _____

06 – Choose Your Inner Circle of Friends Wisely

Journal Prompt #2: *Which relationships in your life feel temporary vs. permanent? Does that affect how you much you will invest in the relationship?*

Date: _____

06 – Choose Your Inner Circle of Friends Wisely

Journal Prompt #3: *Are there any areas of your life where you feel in isolation? Map out a plan for bringing those things into the light and community.*

Date: _____

06 – Choose Your Inner Circle of Friends Wisely

One Month Check-In

Self-reflection and self-discovery are ongoing processes. Use the space below to add a one-month update on your journey.

Date: _____

_____
_____
_____
_____
_____
_____
_____
_____
_____
_____
_____
_____
_____
_____

12 Simple Truths for Living and Loving Yourself

07

Empower Other Women and Girls

"…not looking to your own interests but each of you to the interests of the others."

Philippians 2:4 (NIV)

Live. Love. Grow. Glow.

Empowered women and girls empower other women and girls. Therefore, we need to focus more on building our capacity to be of service to others and love ourselves. Many of us spend countless hours in hair and nail salons, applying make-up, and enhancing our outer appearances, but the real, meaningful, lasting work and growth happens when we invest time and resources working from the inside out. We cannot pour good into the world and empower women and girls when we are attempting to pour from an empty or broken cup. Our cups, namely our minds and bodies, need to not just be full, but filled with the right ingredients. We must be mentally and emotionally healthy, working in harmony with the Holy Spirit, and filled with God's love, faith, forgiveness, patience, kindness, truth, self-acceptance, and self-love so we can empower and uplift other women and girls.

Throughout our lifetimes we are going to encounter women and girls from all walks of life and generations. Understand that these seemingly coincidental encounters are really divinely orchestrated opportunities for us to acknowledge, empower, and celebrate one another. We need to create a culture where women and girls can release assumptions and any inclination to see another woman or girl as a threat or imposition and begin to see each other as sources of empowerment and living examples of God's grace and power. We are not in competition with one another and do not need to dim another woman's or girl's light in order for ours to shine brighter. Our lights are brighter because of the accomplishments and contributions of our mothers, sisters and daughters. We are interconnected on this journey and need to make it a regular practice to honor our elders as if they were our mothers or grandmothers, peers as if they were our sisters, and youth as if they were our very own beloved children.

It is so much easier to judge other people when we do not know their stories and have not connected with them by finding common bonds. Everyone has a story, and if we are not careful, we may focus solely on history and not her-story. Learning about the journeys of other women and girls helps us to make connections on a human and spiritual level and enables us to demonstrate compassion and empathy for one another. Every woman and girl has a story that shaped them into the individuals we see. The stories they share are sprinkled with joy, pain, love, loss, hope, fear, frustrations, and dreams. We need to listen to and learn from the stories and experiences of other women and girls and share our own journeys with the goal of empowerment.

Some of our journeys have been marked by trauma and darkness, which can make it difficult to not only relive those experiences but tell others about them. When this is the case, the lessons learned from the experiences should become the focus of the story. God does not bring us to and through our trials and life experiences for no reason—there is always a greater purpose of which we must be mindful. Our stories are the windows that allow others to peek in and see what is behind the external persona we present to the world and how God has moved and intervened in our lives. Our stories have the potential to be the catalyst that inspires another woman or girl to keep living, loving, growing and finding her purpose.

We need to empower and support each other, and the great thing about it is that there are women and girls right in our families, neighborhoods, and communities that need to hear our stories right now. Women and girls whose paths cross ours need to hear about our personal relationship with God and how we lean into our faith during good and bad times. Women and girls need to hear how we hit the pause button and refocus our energy and attention inward to hear from God when the noise of the world tries to take over and drown out His voice that resides in all of us. They need to hear someone say, "Yes, it is normal to get weary as life can be hard and confusing sometimes, but with the power of God, we can do this. We can always count on God to help us and lean on our faith for strength. God cares and loves you and so do I."

07 – Empower Other Women and Girls

Journal Prompt #1: *What can you do to celebrate, encourage, empower, and support other women and girls? Set a goal that you would like to achieve in one month.*

Date: _____

07 - Empower Other Women and Girls

Journal Prompt #2: *Is there someone you dislike whose story you have failed to learn? Describe some of your encounters with the person and what you dislike. Take some time to listen to her story and perhaps understand the "why" behind her behaviors. What did you learn about the person's story? Did it change your perception?*

Date: _____

07 – Empower Other Women and Girls

Journal Prompt #3: *Who empowers you? In what areas would you like to feel more seen, heard, acknowledged and empowered?*

Date: _____

07 – Empower Other Women and Girls

One Month Check-In

Self-reflection and self-discovery are ongoing processes. Use the space below to add a one-month update on your journey.

Date: _____

_____
_____
_____
_____
_____
_____
_____
_____
_____
_____
_____
_____
_____
_____
_____
_____

12 Simple Truths for Living and Loving Yourself

12 Simple Truths for Living and Loving Yourself

08

Know Your Worth

"For we are God's handiwork, created in Christ Jesus to do good works, which God prepared in advance for us to do."

Ephesians 2:10 (NIV)

Live. Love. Grow. Glow.

When we look at the role of women and girls and how we have been perceived by the dominant male culture and leadership from a historical perspective, we are reminded of how we were, and in some cases still are, seen through a lens of limitations and subordination. We were dismissed, demeaned, and disrespected. We were expected to be seen and not heard. It was believed that we had little to offer, were totally reliant on the males in our lives, and needed to be controlled and managed. We now know for certain that those views were very wrong. Women and girls are invaluable and completely capable of making significant contributions to the world. We have demonstrated our abilities to lead countries, like Vice President Kamala Harris, military organizations, like Lt. Gen. Nadja West, institutions of higher learning, like Dr. Katherine S. Conway-Turner, and communities like Keisha Lance Bottoms and Stacy Abrams. Women and girls have been instrumental in space flight, like Katherine Johnson and Mae Jemison, and risked their lives in the pursuit of freedom and justice, like Malala Yousafzai. Women and girls proved to be vital to the success of many celebrated people, places, and things that have attained notable positions or iconic status. Consider the admiration and respect former president Barack Obama displays towards his wife, Michelle Obama. Whether our good works occur in our homes, churches, at work, our communities, or globally, women and girls empower one another and create pathways for future generations to explore and expand.

Women and girls are the mothers of the Earth. We are an essential life force created by God and called to serve and lead. We should not look to social media, media outlets, government officials, athletes, entertainers, employers, colleagues, or the like to show and tell us who and whose we are. We are God's children and for that reason alone we are valuable and have innate power. The world tends to make us feel invisible, unappreciated, and undervalued, but we do not have to accept that as our reality. Our strength comes from the Lord and while we live in the world, we do not adopt its rules, beliefs, and values as our standards. God's rules are outlined for us in the Bible and revealed to us through His Son Jesus Christ. Jesus is our measuring stick. God loved us so much that He sent His Son not only to die on the cross for our sins, but also to set the example for how we should live our lives. We attach worth or value to our own existence with every word we think, speak and act on each day and with whom we allow to influence our lives. We must remind ourselves every day through positive affirmations and self-talk that we are unique, loved, and valuable--crafted by the very hands that formed Heaven and Earth. One truth that we must never forget is that God loves all of us, women and girls included, so much that we were worth dying for.

08 - Know Your Worth

Journal Prompt #1: *What are you most proud of accomplishing? What legacy would you like to leave the next generation of women and girls? Set a goal that you would like to achieve in one month.*

Date: _____

08 – Know Your Worth

Journal Prompt #2: *How can you add value to other people's lives and make space for other women?*

Date: _____

_____
_____
_____
_____
_____
_____
_____
_____
_____
_____
_____
_____
_____
_____
_____
_____
_____
_____
_____

08 – Know Your Worth

Journal Prompt #3: *If you were to ask God what some of His favorite things are about you, what do you think He would say? His perspective is where your true worth and identity come from!*

Date: _____

08 – Know Your Worth

One Month Check-In

Self-reflection and self-discovery are ongoing processes. Use the space below to add a one-month update on your journey.

Date: _____

_____
_____
_____
_____
_____
_____
_____
_____
_____
_____
_____
_____
_____
_____
_____
_____

09

Practice Self-Discipline

"For the Spirit God gave us does not make us timid, but gives us power, love and self-discipline."

2 Timothy 1:7 (NIV)

Live. Love. Grow. Glow.

Self-discipline is an important trait that we must develop over time. It should be among the priority items on our self-improvement lists. Self-discipline requires lifestyle changes to which we must commit. Qualities exhibited by people who practice self-discipline include self-control, clear focus, persistence, resilience, humility, responsibility, a strong work ethic, healthy routines, and graciousness.

As we live our lives, it is important for us to practice spiritual disciplines that will enable us to master self-discipline. Spiritual disciplines that many people find helpful include prayer, focused and relaxed breathing, journaling, reading, and meditation to reduce stress and refocus back to the Holy Spirit. Others find it beneficial to recite positive affirmations and engage in positive self-talk. Creating boundaries and devoting time for quiet are also common practices. Establishing healthy routines is essential to developing the skills required for self-discipline and strategically managing the constant pressing and pulling of outside forces that want to dictate how we spend our time, what we think about, and what we hold dear. Practicing self-discipline enables us to move in ways that more closely align with God's will for our lives.

When we lack self-discipline, we often find it more difficult to focus on what is important. We lose sight of the fact that as children of God we are to bear some resemblance to His character, leading us to act and react in ways that are not God-honoring. Undeveloped self-discipline negatively impacts our ability to communicate our needs effectively and keep our priorities in order. Sometimes when I am watching TV or looking online, I see the behaviors people, oftentimes parents, are engaging in, and I just cringe because I am keenly aware of the negative impact these exploits will have on society as a whole. A concerning number of people, youth and adults alike, appear to be on a path of self-destruction, living as if there is no hope, no tomorrow, and no consequences for the choices they make. Those of us who know the Lord recognize that where we spend eternity is on the line and we will have to give an account for every idle word and action.

We need God to step in and empower us to develop self-discipline and model behaviors that are God-honoring and reflective of His character. Adults who lack good judgment, self-control, self-respect, and have little or no regard for human life typically raise children who follow their examples. Educators often see the impact a lack of self-discipline has on individuals firsthand. We see children coming to school weighed down mentally and emotionally by the realities of their worlds and functioning in survival mode as a result of adverse childhood experiences. They present as withdrawn, angry, depressed, confused, anxious and hopeless. These children are in desperate need of role models who will protect them and help them develop self-regulation, or coping skills, as they try to make sense of the world. They need adults in their villages who have adequately dealt with their own traumas; these are the ones who can then teach them about a loving and ever-present God and demonstrate how self-discipline is lived out. How can we reasonably expect our young people to develop these skills if we as the adults and role models in their lives have not mastered them ourselves? Our children need to know that there is hope and peace available for them when they choose to follow God's will; that message needs to be communicated through the words and actions of adults.

We must each develop our own personal relationship with God and grow our faith. We have to get our priorities straight and ensure that we are setting those in our villages up for success and not repeating unhealthy behaviors and habits that have been passed down through generations in our own families and communities. Practicing self-discipline and accessing God through Jesus Christ is a conscious choice we need to make for ourselves, our families, our communities, and particularly those who depend on us for guidance and direction.

God knows us and loves us despite our shortcomings. He is simply waiting for us to use the free will granted to all of us to choose Him. We can change course, if necessary, by first developing a personal relationship with God and trusting Him with our lives. He will take over from there and provide the roadmap and skills we need for our journey. We are called to be living examples of God's love, grace, and mercy, and practicing self-discipline is a prerequisite skill.

09 – Practice Self-Discipline

Journal Prompt #1: *What are some of the ways you demonstrate self-discipline? Which spiritual disciplines do you practice routinely? What is a spiritual discipline you would like to introduce into your daily routines and why? Set a goal that you would like to achieve in one month.*

Date: _____

09 – Practice Self-Discipline

Journal Prompt #2: *Are there any lifestyle adjustments that God is leading you to make in order to be more focused on His plan for your life?*

Date: _____

09 – Practice Self-Discipline

Journal Prompt #3: *What is one aspect of God's character that you are inspired by? How can self-discipline help you to move towards seeing this more fully in your own life?*

Date: _____

_____
_____
_____
_____
_____
_____
_____
_____
_____
_____
_____
_____
_____
_____
_____

09 – Practice Self-Discipline

One Month Check-In

Self-reflection and self-discovery are ongoing processes. Use the space below to add a one-month update on your journey.

Date: _____

12 Simple Truths for Living and Loving Yourself

10

Speak Your Truth

"My words come from an upright heart; My lips sincerely speak what I know."

Job 33:3 (NIV)

Live. Love. Grow. Glow.

Speaking the truth in love is an example of using the power of words as a catalyst in our pursuit to becoming the most authentic and best versions of ourselves. The ultimate goal of speaking our truth is to be able to honor our feelings and share the difficult parts of our stories in a manner that is direct, loving, and kind, yet gets the message across. We must learn to find our voices and become skilled at communicating our needs, wants, and what we require to different people in a variety of contexts. We have to learn to advocate for ourselves and give our dreams, feelings and plans a voice.

Words are one of the most powerful forces we possess. Our words contain a great deal of energy that can be used to encourage and enlighten or divide and dismiss. The Bible tells us in Proverbs 18:21, "The tongue has the power of life and death, and those who love it will eat its fruits." With this in mind, we must learn to choose our words wisely and remember that truth and love go hand in hand.

When speaking our truth in love, we must also be aware of what we are communicating nonverbally--through our tone and our body language. Our ability to communicate effectively reflects our character, spiritual maturity, and desire for unity with others in God's kingdom. It is important for there to be alignment between our words and the values that we hold dear because we should endeavor to draw others to Christ, not push them away. As comfortable or uncomfortable as it may feel, speaking the truth in love is required in order to be an honest and authentic person, achieve our goals, walk in faith, and stand in our purpose. We must learn to speak our truth, choose our words wisely, and understand the direct relationship between our words, our reality, and our results.

10 – Speak Your Truth

Journal Prompt #1: *How can you improve your ability to speak your truth in a manner that honors your feelings and preserves the message and dignity of all parties? Set a goal that you would like to achieve in one month.*

Date: _____

10 – Speak Your Truth

Journal Prompt #2: *What needs to be said that you have not yet said and to whom? What keeps you from speaking your truth?*

Date: _____

10 – Speak Your Truth

Journal Prompt #3: *What are some relational needs that you have? Take some time to assess, then communicate them to the people closest to you.*

Date: _____

10 – Speak Your Truth

One Month Check-In

Self-reflection and self-discovery are ongoing processes. Use the space below to add a one-month update on your journey.

Date: _____

12 Simple Truths for Living and Loving Yourself

11

Seek Peace and Justice for All

"Learn to do right; seek justice. Defend the oppressed. Take up the cause of the fatherless; plead the case of the widow."

Isaiah 1:17 (NIV)

Live. Love. Grow. Glow.

Our nation and world look to be in chaos right now and people are sick, hungry, hurting, and lost. There seems to be a pervasive lack of compassion and direction, and many people are focused solely on selfish pursuits. We do not respect differences, nor do we value life. Many of us have lost our way and are looking in all the wrong places for guidance, answers, and peace. Many of us are confused and hurting and in turn, are hurting others.

According to Proverbs 6:16-19, there are seven things that God hates: arrogant eyes, a lying tongue, hands that shed innocent blood, a heart that devises wicked schemes, feet that are quick to rush to evil, a false witness who pours out lies, and a person who stirs up conflict in the community. These very things are rampant in our society today. We have lost perspective and our priorities and values are out of order and alignment with the Holy Spirit and foundational Christian principles. For example, the root of hate and racism is spiritual, so its fix must be spiritual as well.

We have to redefine how we discern and define right and wrong and look to scripture, which is God-breathed and useful for teaching and correcting, to deal with every situation. There is a biblical principle that speaks to everything we are facing and answers every question we have. We may be surprised by the things people say and do and events that occur, but nothing comes as a surprise to God. He remains in control and awaits the day we decide to do things His way and in His power. The Bible is waiting for us to open it, read it, and apply its principles to our lives. We have to drown out the forces of evil that seem to have occupied the spirits and minds of far too many of us. God's word is true and His way is the only way. We are commanded to fear God, keep away from evil, be salt and light on the Earth, be peacemakers, and keep God's commandments. Yes, we were each given free will, which allows us the freedom to make choices about how we live our lives, who we listen to, and who we follow; however, we can never lose sight of the fact that we will answer for our actions and our choices when we meet God face to face one day.

Social justice and peace will become a reality when we accept the gift of Salvation offered through Jesus Christ. There is no pain, sorrow, or situation that Jesus did not experience during His time on Earth that we are experiencing now. He gets it. He feels our pain and understands our struggles. Most importantly, He loves us and gave His life to save us from our sins. We must model our lives after God's blueprint in order for the idea of one nation, under God, indivisible, with liberty and justice, and peace for all to become a reality. The same way God extends us grace and mercy, we have to do the same for one another. We must see others as God sees them and us. When we look at God's two greatest commandments, we see our mission in clear and concise terms: that we love the Lord our God with all our heart and with all our soul and with all our mind and love our neighbors as ourselves (Matthew 22:37-39).

Countless generations before us fought valiantly to obtain and protect rights that should be afforded to all human beings, often losing their lives, limbs, possessions, and loved ones in the process. They fought and sacrificed for us for the same reason Jesus died on the cross for us— because they loved us. We too must join the fight for justice and lead those who have not accepted the gift of salvation to God through His Son Jesus Christ. Future generations are relying on us to be peacemakers, to right wrongs, and do our part to create a world where the common good is the common goal. We should be able to enjoy a peaceful life where we are not limited, silenced, or threatened because of our gender, race, economic status, or religious beliefs. Jesus came as the Son of man to serve and not to be served, so we too must do our part to serve others, being a voice for the voiceless and oppressed. Let us fulfill our divine purpose as salt and light in the world.

11 – Seek Peace and Justice for All

Journal Prompt #1: *In what ways can you serve others and encourage peace and justice for all? Set a goal that you would like to achieve in one month.*

Date: _____

11 – Seek Peace and Justice for All

Journal Prompt #2: *What injustices have you experienced or witnessed? How does this inform your sense of purpose?*

Date: _____

11 – Seek Peace and Justice for All

Journal Prompt #3: *What are some basic human rights that should be afforded to every human being? What does the Bible say about these things?*

Date: _____

11 – Seek Peace and Justice for All

One Month Check-In

Self-reflection and self-discovery are ongoing processes. Use the space below to add a one-month update on your journey.

Date: _____

_____
_____
_____
_____
_____
_____
_____
_____
_____
_____
_____
_____
_____
_____
_____
_____
_____

12

Be the Best Version of Yourself

"Finally brothers and sisters, whatever is true, whatever is noble, whatever is right, whatever is pure, whatever is lovely, whatever is admirable-if anything is excellent or praiseworthy-think about such things."

Philippians 4:8 (NIV)

Live. Love. Grow. Glow.

As we move through the stages of life, all we can really do is our best and learn the lessons life is teaching us each step along the way. We should continually seek wisdom and understanding, beginning with Biblical truths. We must make goal-setting on spiritual, personal, and professional levels an integral part of our lives. We also need to learn from the stories and examples of others and share our own experiences.

To become the best version of ourselves, we must center our lives authentically around God's will for our lives and the purpose and passions He has instilled in us. Every experience and person we encounter along our life journey is divinely orchestrated and intended to encourage this self-reflection and self-discovery. The goal is to make better choices with greater wisdom as we progress and grow into the women God has created us to be.

In this journey of evolving, we must first learn to love and forgive ourselves. Our mistakes and misfortunes do not define us, nor do they make us less lovable or worthy of respect. We have to learn to forgive ourselves for past mistakes and release any anger or resentment we are harboring towards others. These built-up emotions will only become more and more toxic over time, separating us from God and destroying us from the inside out. We have to remember that there are no perfect people, and our personal growth and learning to love ourselves is a life-long process. Each day that God allows us to live is a fresh opportunity to live according to His will. God is full of grace and mercy, giving us multiple chances to repair what we have broken and align our will with His. As long as we have breath in our bodies, hope is alive.

We should then seek to surround ourselves with like-minded people who love and know God for themselves. This Godly accountability equips us to become an example for other women and girls who have yet to learn about God's love and salvation through Jesus Christ. Women and girls must make the personal commitment to love and encourage one another and to be kind, grateful, disciplined, intentional, and authentic.

Motherhood ignited my journey to becoming the best version of myself, and my children continue to play a vital role in those efforts as they enter adulthood. It quickly became real to me from the time I found out I was going to be a mother, that I was taking on an enormous responsibility. I knew that children were gifts from God and each time I felt the little kicks and hiccups, I was reminded that He was entrusting me with His most precious gift. When I held my babies for the first time and looked into those innocent, beautiful little faces, I recognized the miracle that had occurred. The love and emotions that poured over me when I held my babies left me speechless. My protective instincts kicked in, and I immediately became committed to protecting their mental, physical, spiritual, and emotional well-being. I thanked God for entrusting me with these little girls and gladly accepted the responsibility of preparing them for their journeys through life, beginning with establishing a foundation built on faith and Christian principles. I dedicated my life to serving my daughters and giving them the best life that I could with an understanding that it was not about how much money or how many material things I could provide, but rather how I would be the best mom so that they could be their best.

So much of what we know and who we become is dependent on the example set by members of the villages that raise us. We all start off as tiny little sponges, full of awe, hopes, and dreams. We are being shaped by everything we see and hear, particularly from the women and girls in our lives. There is always someone younger, older, or around the same age and stage watching and learning from our actions. As a result, we must continually strive to be the best versions of ourselves, which in turn will lead others to do the same. We must acknowledge the responsibility we have to the people in the spaces we occupy and equip them with the knowledge, experiences, and spiritual guidance they need to be successful in this life. We must accept the charge to be salt and light in our own homes, communities, and amongst our peers, as indicated in Matthew 5:13-16.

Life is happening all around us at a very fast pace. We never know what tomorrow is going to bring. What we do know is that the Bible teaches us that we are known by our actions, so we must continually examine and align them with our Godly purpose. We must do everything we can, while we can, to set ourselves and others up for success and ensure that we leave a legacy that will matter in eternity.

12 – Be the Best Version of Yourself

Journal Prompt #1: *In what areas can you love yourself better? Do you need to forgive yourself or anyone for events from the past? Set a goal that you would like to accomplish in one month.*

Date: _____

12 – Be the Best Version of Yourself

Journal Prompt #2: *Take a moment to assess your strengths. What qualities do people admire about you? What can you do to show up more fully in your areas of strength?*

Date: _____

12 – Be the Best Version of Yourself

Journal Prompt #3: *Take a moment to assess a few of your weaknesses. How can you transform your weaknesses into strengths so that you can be the best version of yourself?*

Date: _____

_____
_____
_____
_____
_____
_____
_____
_____
_____
_____
_____
_____
_____
_____
_____
_____
_____
_____
_____

12 – Be the Best Version of Yourself

One Month Check-In

Self-reflection and self-discovery are ongoing processes. Use the space below to add a one-month update on your journey.

Date: _____

12 Simple Truths for Living and Loving Yourself

Dear Reader,

You have concluded this part of the journey to self-love, self-reflection, and self-discovery. This process is an ongoing one with multiple pathways to self-actualization. Your journey will need to continue as future generations of women and girls are relying on you to set the example for living a bold, brilliant, and blessed life. In a world that does not always nurture or protect the infinite potential of the next generation, may you arise as the new standard of elders. We are all elders to someone and have a responsibility to show them that they are loved, valued, and fearfully and wonderfully made by God, the Creator of all good and perfect things. It is never too soon or too late to make a positive difference in someone's life or change the course of your own. You matter. Your experiences matter. Your story matters.

I have found that age and experience do not make you a wise person; self-reflection, intentionality, and learning from the lessons life teaches make you wise. My hope is that some of these simple truths spoke to your heart and inspired you to love yourself more, dream bigger, and shine brighter. Remember, empowered women and girls empower other women and girls to live, love, grow, and glow. They let their lights shine so that others may see their good works and glorify God. Make a positive difference in the spaces you occupy by sharing your story and learned lessons.

12 Simple Truths for Living and Loving Yourself

Journal

12 Simple Truths for Living and Loving Yourself

Journal

12 Simple Truths for Living and Loving Yourself

Journal

12 Simple Truths for Living and Loving Yourself

Journal

12 Simple Truths for Living and Loving Yourself

Journal

12 Simple Truths for Living and Loving Yourself

Journal

12 Simple Truths for Living and Loving Yourself

Journal

About the Author

Lisa Lynch is an educator, author, daughter, wife, mother, sister, niece, cousin, aunt, great-aunt, and friend. Her debut book, *12 Simple Truths for Living and Loving Yourself: A Journey of Self-Reflection and Self-Discovery for Women and Girls*, is the first in a collection of guided journals written to educate and inspire the next generation of girls and to remind women of God's love and desire for them to rely on Him, embrace their power, and live purposeful, fulfilling lives as the best versions of themselves.

Lisa enjoys reading, writing, traveling, sports, yoga, teaching, learning, and spending time with family and friends. She resides in Virginia with her husband, daughters, and mother.

12 Simple Truths for Living and Loving Yourself

Live.

Love.

Grow.

Glow.

Matthew 5:16

www.ingramcontent.com/pod-product-compliance
Lightning Source LLC
Chambersburg PA
CBHW030911080526
44589CB00010B/258